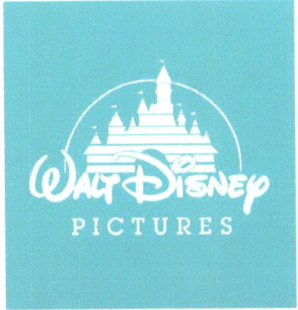

THE "B" WORD

Becoming foolishly bold in creating
the ultimate "brand"

by Bobby Marhamat

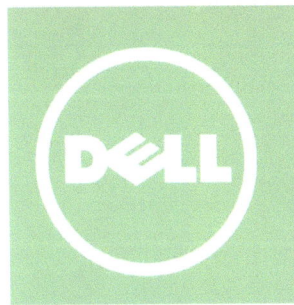
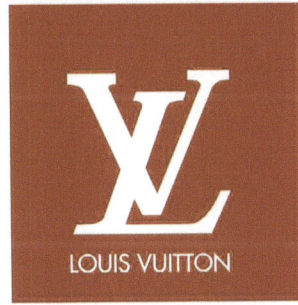
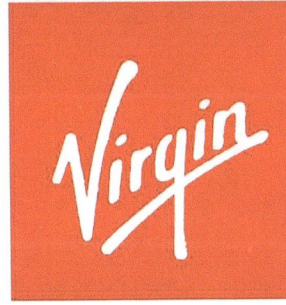

"Life is a game and there are many ways to keep score. Stick with your gut, reward your hard work with hard play, and you'll find yourself on top of the leaderboards. Building a brand is all about the vision and drive that goes into your day - both professionally and socially."

- Bobby Marhamat

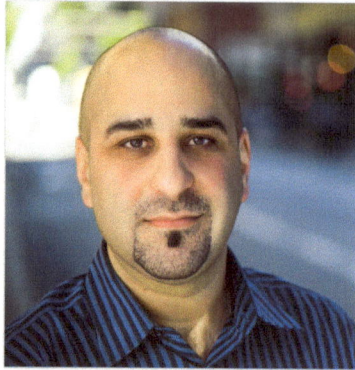

Bobby Marhamat

About the Author

Before I start rambling, I want you to get to know me. So I pieced together a quick bio to walk you through my career thus far.

I have always been an entrepreneur at heart. In fact, I created my first company when I was nine years old. I have helped many companies and business owners look at different ways to make more money by unifying their brand and creating a niche within their target market.

I have worked with and increased exposure and ROI for a number of fortune 500 companies', including Sprint Nextel, Looksmart, Neiman Marcus, Macy's and Verizon Wireless EVO² - not to forget about the hundreds of small business owners that I have taught how to peel away the old layers in their business - with a clear focus on branding themselves to the top.

So I welcome you to the world of branding - and the direct affect it will have on your business' existence.

THE "B" WORD

Becoming foolishly bold in creating the ultimate "brand"

by Bobby Marhamat

Copyright © 2013 by Bobby Marhamat

Table of Contents

INTRODUCTION

What would you say your customers envision when they hear your company name? What goes through their minds when they see your logo? Does your answer to either of those questions make you…uncomfortable?

Your company is more than the sum of its parts. It's more than the design printed on your business cards or hanging on the sign above your front door. Your company's brand extends far beyond the borders of your shop, past the marketing materials you distribute, or even the products and services you sell.

Let's think about this. What do you think of when you hear names like these?

- Nike
- Apple
- Kashi

Chances are good you think of more than running shoes, computers and electronics or a bowl of cereal. Nike is synonymous with fitness, pushing the limits and bettering yourself through effort. Apple connotes innovation, forward thinking and beautiful, evocative design that goes beyond their consumer electronics and becomes part of their customers' lives. Kashi is renowned for more than just healthy cereals – the company evokes ties back to the way life used to be, exploration and the quest for the highest quality.

The same thing applies to your company. Whether you sell shoes or paper products, electronics or housewares, your company is much more than just the sum of its various parts in the minds of your customers. Branding is the key to building the image you want in the minds of your customers and clients.

Each of the companies listed above has successfully engaged in positive branding and created a presence that extends far beyond the boundaries of their physical stores or product shelves and made them part of their customers' actual lives.
You can do this, too.

With the right branding and the right mindset, you can build a company reputation, a business image and a culture that not only connects with those who matter most, but also allows you to become much more than just another faceless, anonymous business. This book is designed to arm you with all the information you need to understand what branding is all about, how to get started, and make informed and powerful decisions about your branding campaigns and overall strategy.

Not only that, but this book will guide you through the process of actually understanding what your brand truly is – a vital consideration for any business, regardless of industry or niche. Without a real understanding of brand, it's impossible to build the respect, reputation and relationships with customers' necessary to not only survive, but to prosper in this competitive modern world.

Branding is vital, but it can also be fun and rewarding. What's more – you don't have to be another Apple or Nike to do it. Every business owner or entrepreneur can achieve tremendous success here. You just need to know what to do.

1 WHAT THE HECK IS BRANDING?

To help you make the most of your efforts, we need to start at the very beginning. Branding is at once both a simple and complex concept. It's as simple as the emotion you feel when you see a well-known brand's logo, and as complex as the steps taken by companies to ensure their message gets out there through social media, traditional marketing and other advertising methods. So, what is branding? This chapter will provide you a good foundation in the topic.

What's in a Brand?

First, let's look at what a brand actually is. According to Wikipedia, a brand is: "A name, term, design, symbol or any other feature that identifies on seller's good or service as distinct from those of other sellers."

That definition gives us some important information:

- Your brand is MORE THAN your products or service
- Your brand is MORE THAN your company
- Your brand is MORE THAN your customer service
- Your brand is MORE THAN your marketing efforts
- Your brand is MORE THAN your company's culture, history or roots

So, if your brand is more than these things, how are you supposed to go about effectively branding your business? It can be a little difficult. A good brand combines a wide range of potential elements, stretching from the physical to the ephemeral.

For instance, Kentucky Fried Chicken's brand includes their trademarked 11-spice mixture, but it's really the flavor of the company's chicken that comes across in their marketing campaigns. It's not the chicken itself, but the experience of sinking your teeth into that chicken evoked by marketing in the minds of their customers.

Understand the Elements

Numerous other elements go into a brand in order to summon elements of your company's culture and quality in your customers' minds. For instance, your actual logo is a considerable part, as is the company's name. Another element is graphic design (think the Coca-Cola ribbon or Nike's "swoosh"). Colors, shapes and taglines are also components here.

The point is that your brand can vary considerably from all other companies in your niche or industry and still be evocative and compelling. This brings us back to the question of what is branding?

Branding

Branding is the act of enhancing brand awareness, of defining your brand's identity. You control this process, which is a good thing. It allows you to create a brand identity and awareness that matches your goals and helps you engender the emotional response in customers/clients that you want. However, let's not get ahead of ourselves.

Branding is not the same thing as marketing your products or services; it's not advertising, nor is it PR work. Essentially, it's building your platform, and if it's not done correctly, all the marketing expertise – and dollars – in the world won't help you.

Bobby Marhamat

At its heart, branding is a conversation between you and your customers. It's about influencing how they truly perceive you and what they say about your company once they're no longer on the sales floor. It's about culture, personality and lifestyle. That's a lot to pack into any business image, but it can be done if you take the time to understand the process and what you should (and shouldn't) do.

"Perhaps the most salient factor for the most successful brands is the promise of consistent quality. Whether it's a business or a consumer making a purchasing decision, they want to be sure in this world of endless choice that their decision is the right one."
– Rosi McMurray, Executive Director of Strategy, The Brand Union

Bobby Marhamat

2 FOCUS YOUR FOCUS

Whatever your company offers, it's vital that you have a niche and that you focus on building your brand within that niche. Niche branding offers a means to gain better traction for small businesses that cannot compete against the marketing budgets of the big boys.

Gatorade – A Brief Case Study

As with most things, an example of niche focus can provide invaluable insight. One of the best recent niche campaigns focuses can be found with the powerhouse sports drink company, Gatorade. The recent spate of TV commercials, print ads and even online marketing from the company has focused almost exclusively on what Gatorade can do for the company's target audience – sports players.

A closer look at the ads will reveal that the company's message doesn't focus on their products, but on how their products solve a problem for their customers. In sports, those problems are dehydration and better performance.

Within the ads, this is done by minimizing the focus on the product (the drinks) and increasing the focus on players overcoming exhaustion and dehydration to "up their game" after drinking Gatorade. This is accompanied by text that focuses on their audiences need, including:

- Own the first move
- Sustain your game

- Energy to fuel athletes
- Keep her in the game
- Win from within

This focus on solving problems immediately connects with the company's target audience in a way impossible to do by focusing strictly on the product itself. High profile sports figures are used to connect with the rest of us – their customers

Defining Niche Focus

There are many different types of branding. Broad-scope branding is the most common – think of the AdSense ads we encounter on websites, the Facebook ads we run into while surfing the social network and the vast majority of commercials everyone suffers through while watching television.

Niche focus branding is very different. To understand this, let's focus a bit more on what the term actually means.

Niche Focus – Also known as "narrow branding," it focuses on connecting with your audience in a targeted way that shows your company can meet their needs, solve their problem or help in their situation. It isn't focused on your products, however; it's focused on your customers. In a way, it's a lot like social media marketing. It removes the focus from your company and places it squarely on the target audience, which is very different from traditional marketing.

Developing Your Focus

Now that we have touched briefly on how niche focus differs from traditional broad-based marketing efforts, it's time to look at how you actually develop your focus. There are specific steps that you must take in order to adequately identify your audience and determine what their needs are, to concentrate on meeting those needs.

- **Step 1:** The first step is research. You must know who your target audience is. Who is your average customer? Does your product appeal to business owners? Do you sell to sports players? Is there a specific professional demographic you need to reach?

  Defining your target audience allows you to cut out the vast majority of people who won't benefit from your product and narrow your focus to just those who are most likely to need what you have to offer. Targeted marketing is nothing new, and you'll find these connotations used in many different areas.

- **Step 2:** How will you reach these people? Determining how your company, product or service will be introduced to your audience is important for several reasons. First, some methods are more invasive – and costly – than others, such as direct mail marketing, for example. Others, like Facebook ads, are very passive.

  To really understand the answer to this question, you have to think like your target audience, and put yourself in their shoes. If you were in their position, where would you first encounter your brand? Where would it do THEM the most good to be introduced to your offerings?

  Take a bit of time to put yourself in your customers' position and you'll begin to find a range of locations and ways to introduce your solution to their problems.

- **Step 3:** Think like your customers. What problems do they face? All products should be created to fill a definite need. If your product or service doesn't, then it might be time to go back to the drawing board. Determine exactly what problems your audience faces and how you can meet that need.

  To use Gatorade as an example once more, the need is greater performance in their sport while combating dehydration. Again, put yourself into your customers' position. What problems would you experience in their shoes?

- **Step 4:** How do you solve those problems? Now that you have a better idea of the problems and situations your audience faces, what does your product or service to do alleviate those issues? What benefits does that product offer? How does your service meet their needs while differing from the competition?

  You might be more familiar with this as "USP", or unique selling proposition, and it really boils down to how you can benefit your audience (which is why they would buy what you're offering in the first place).

- **Step 5:** How do you trump the competition? Now that you know the problems faced by your target market and how your product answers those needs, it's time to turn to the question of how you differ from your competition. In some ways, this is as important as how you meet your customers' needs; determine exactly how your offerings differ from your competitors.

Relationship Building – The Real Focus in Niche Branding

Interestingly, niche branding has a lot in common with social media marketing. Both share a focus on what you can do for your audience. Both focus on benefits, rather than pushing your product. Additionally, both focus on developing relationships. One of what really sets niche branding apart from other forms of branding. If you're not focusing on building relationships with your audience, your efforts will be less effective than otherwise.

Creating a real relationship with your audience is vital for a number of reasons, including creating the optimum impression of your company. In a sense, building the right impression or view of your company and your products or services with your target audience is the entire purpose of niche branding. It's about creating a lasting, positive image.

It's about building relationships so that when your customers realize they have a problem, your company or product is the first thing that comes to mind. Again, Gatorade is a great example of this – what would you rather have on the field or the court, a soda or something that replenishes what you've lost and gives you an edge?

Bobby Marhamat

"True cultural connection is the Holy Grail for brands if they want to create an enduring emotional relationship with people."
– Adam Chmielowski, Flamingo

3 WHAT'S THE WORD?

Who are you most likely to take your car to for repairs, someone who just opened their shop or a mechanic with a track record of performance that specializes in repairing vehicles like yours? Don't answer: You'll go to the specialist, and for good reason.

We all want to work with an expert, which is one reason so many self-styled "gurus" have found success. Don't worry about becoming a guru, but effective branding does require that you build a reputation for expertise and knowledge.

Google – A Brief Case Study

You want to find more information about a topic. Perhaps you want to find out more about running shoes, or maybe you're expecting a new baby and want to find out what the top brands are for furniture to outfit the nursery. Where do you turn?

Almost universally, for most of us, the answer is "Google".

Google has positioned itself as the leading Internet search engine by doing one thing very well and better than anyone else – proving their ability to deliver real results. They're the industry-leader in virtually every way, from market share to page hits per day around the world.

Google has done an amazing job of positioning themselves as experts in the search industry. That effort has translated into lasting, rather astounding results. You need to do the same thing

– you must gain expertise in your industry or niche, and then give it away, building a reputation as an industry leader.

You'll find very little direct marketing for Google – the company doesn't need it. Where else are you going to turn? Would you prefer to use Bing, Yahoo or Ask.com? For most people, the answer is no. And there are good reasons for this:

- Google's results are more accurate.
- Google's results are more expansive.
- Google offers free information on virtually everything, including how to use the company's programs (like AdSense) to your own benefit.
- Google goes to great lengths to connect with their audience (which is pretty much everyone) through blogs, new initiatives and free offerings that provide real value.
- Google is also a green company, with a wide range of sustainable initiatives that reduce the company's carbon footprint, so the firm can be seen as striving for a better future for humanity.

Ways to Build Expertise

Now that you can see the benefits of building expertise and positioning yourself as a thought leader within your industry or niche, it's time to tackle a more difficult question.

How do you do that?

You can take cues from almost every industry on the planet, all of which harbor thought leaders, innovators and experts. However, this section will detail some of the most important things for you to do in order to lead your industry and brand yourself as an "expert".

Be Dedicated to Innovation

Innovation is one of the hottest "buzzwords" today, but it's been bandied about so often and so casually that much of its meaning has been lost. Gurus are constantly lobbying their audience to "be innovators" and to "dream big", but there's much more to innovation than that.

Innovation is defined as, "the development of new customers value through solutions that meet new needs, inarticulate needs, or old customer and market needs in new ways".

That definition holds the key to innovating in terms of your business – it's about meeting the needs of your customers (you should be starting to see a trend here). It's not about pushing your products or new forms of marketing. It's not about new ways to get your name out to the masses. Innovation is about meeting needs and solving problems through new methods, products or services.

In order to be an industry leader or expert, you need to be focused on maintaining innovation within your business. That means you cannot be content to "rest on your laurels". The moment forward movement stops within your company, you stop leading the industry. Want an example of this? Take a good look at how Apple's products have continued to evolve.

Apple is a company never been content with their current generation of products. They constantly ask how those products can be made better, how they can better meet their customers' needs. While not every new iPod, iPhone, iPad or Mac Book iteration will be a colossal hit, they all represent forward momentum in the race to anticipate and meet real needs.

Invest in Ongoing Education

Lifelong learners already know a big secret: More knowledge is always a good thing, and that there's always something new you can learn. This can be applied directly to your efforts to build expertise and the impression that your company leads the industry. By focusing on ongoing education and training, you ensure that you, your employees and your company remain on the leading edge of your niche.

Let's look at it another way. Would you prefer to let a mechanic whose education was limited to working on 1970's muscle cars repair your hybrid? That would be a bad idea. However, if that same mechanic invested in ongoing training and education through ASE testing and certification courses, he would have the skills necessary to repair any modern vehicle, as well as older cars.

You are that mechanic. The cars you repair are the needs of your customers. By investing in ongoing education and training, you ensure that you stay abreast of current developments in terms of technology, manufacturing, operating principles and more. That isn't limited to manufacturers, either.

Even if your business is a local shoe store, ongoing training can help you learn how to better meet the needs of your customers, engendering a reputation for expertise and excellence. For example, new technologies, materials and manufacturing methods evolve constantly in the athletic footwear world. By staying current with these advances, you can provide customers in need of better performance, stability or support with exactly what they need.

If you think that ongoing education has to be time consuming and expensive, it's time to look at your options again. It can be as simple as subscribing to industry periodicals, other leading blogs and staying abreast of industry news from manufacturers.

Give Information Away

One of the best ways to build a reputation for expertise and excellence is to give information away to your audience. Google is an excellent example of this simple and effective strategy. The Official Google Blog is a great place to find a very wide range of information, from details about upcoming products the company is involved with to tips about using their platforms to the best effect and more. You can do something similar.

Setting up a blog is a very good way to give valuable information to your audience free of charge. It's simple, can be tied to your company's website and can also be linked to your social media accounts for better information dissemination and traffic generation. However, you don't have to use technology to benefit from it; even those who wouldn't know a blog from a Twitter account can still position themselves as experts by offering information to customers. Leaflets, brochures and even just informal discussions with customers who walk through your doors can do the trick.

Focus on What Matters

Building expertise in your industry or niche implies several things, including developing skills or expertise in specific areas. As a business owner, chances are good that you have a wide range of skills in disparate areas, but those areas are not all created equal.

For instance, your skills with accounting probably won't wow your customers. However, your knowledge of advanced sole construction materials might just do the trick for customers in search of new footwear. Your knowledge of heavy machinery lifespan and utility will matter to construction industry customers.

The point is that there are specific areas that should be developed – those areas are the ones of supreme importance to your customers or client base. If you've done your due diligence in niche branding, then you already know who your customers are, where they are and what their needs are. Focus your expertise-building efforts on skills that directly touch on those needs.

"Unless you have absolute clarity of what your brand stands for, everything else is irrelevant."

– Mark Baynes, Global CMO, Kellogg Co.

4 | TALK, TALK, TALK

Building your brand requires conversation. While much of that conversation should center on your customers and potential customers, you also need to tie in your services or products. This can be done in several ways, and it doesn't have to be blatant marketing. There are more effective ways to promote what you offer than clubbing people over the head with advertising.

Cadbury – A Brief Case Study

When it comes to creating conversation, there are few tools as powerful as Twitter. Cadbury, the famed chocolate candy company, learned this firsthand when they discontinued one of their chocolate bars. The outpouring of support from loyal fans in favor of the company bringing back the candy bar was overwhelming, and the company chose to engage in conversation about their decision to do just that.

Cadbury used Twitter to build a following of the most outspoken fans of their products, and then engaged with them about the rerelease of the candy bar. The immediate result was an awareness campaign centering around conversation about the company's products – a two-way conversation between Cadbury and their customers and fans allowing the company to promote their products and do it without traditional advertising. Those Twitter fans then spread the message, creating an awareness campaign that provided very substantial results.

You can enjoy the same benefits by creating a conversation around your products or services, how they fit your customers' needs and more. However, there are a few things that you'll need to know before leaping straight in here.

Talk the Talk but Cut Out the Sales

The first thing you need to understand about this type of brand building is that it's not overt marketing. That's at odds with the way many business owners think, but it's imperative that you don't drown them with your marketing messages. You need to change your mindset here; this is the time to engage, rather than hard sell.

Take a page from the social media marketing playbook. If you're new to that particular medium, here's a quick crash course on the do's and don'ts:

- Do: Engage in actual conversation with fans, friends, and followers
- Don't: Spout nothing but ads or links to your products
- Do: Share and promote others
- Don't: Bash competitors for any reason – even if you're tempted
- Do: Answer questions or concerns, particularly if they are about your products or touch on something your product or service can help with
- Don't: Blatantly promote yourself for no reason at all
- Social media isn't the time for shameless self-promotion, and neither is your branding

While those tips are taken straight from social media marketing, they can apply to virtually any brand building effort, including engaging potential customers in real conversation. You'll notice a recurring theme in the tips listed above – there's no direct selling allowed. That's important to understand.

Why Direct Selling in Conversation Is Bad

Here's the thing. If you don't see a problem with selling during an actual conversation, you're doing it wrong. You're taking things too far. You've gone from being a valuable resource to being little more than a spammer (even in real life conversation). Most people have a healthy (well-deserved) distrust for marketers.

However, there are ways that you can insert your message in your conversations without having people eventually avoid you.

- Address actual problems and situations when your product can help.
- Engage in conversation about the industry, and position yourself up as a leader within that industry.
- Engage your customers in conversation about how and where they use your products.
- Speak with your customers and potential customers about their actual needs.
- Empathize with them and make reasoned suggestions that include your products.

Direct selling must be avoided if you want to really create a feeling of trust. You have to be recognized for providing value in all things, not for one-sided conversations that center only on you.

The Importance of Blogging

In the last chapter, we touched on blogging and its importance in building expertise and positioning yourself as a thought leader. However, it's also an invaluable conversation tool, and you can use it very easily to market your products or services.

Blogging has rapidly become one of the most vital tools available to brand builders since it emerged on the scene years ago. That importance hasn't faded with the rise of social media. Rather, it might actually be the just the opposite.

Your blog is an ideal way to share stories and information from real customers and clients that attest to the value and quality of what you offer, without actually engaging in direct marketing. It's also a great way to engender conversation through posts about your industry, processes or materials specific to your products, tips for consumers and more.

Go Social

This chapter has mentioned social media more than once, and now it's time to go a bit more in-depth with it. If you're not involved with social media at least to some extent, you're missing a powerful branding tool. From Facebook to LinkedIn, Twitter and G+ (to say nothing of the hundreds of other sites out there), social media is an important consideration for any company looking to build their brand and engage their audience in conversation.

Where and how do you do that, though? The four social networks listed above are the best places to start. However, remember the tips listed previously – be authentic, engage in real conversation and avoid direct marketing tactics. Be real and enjoyable and your audience will reward you by wanting to spend time with your brand.

Bobby Marhamat

"Brands are not ends in themselves; they're a solution, something that allows us to achieve something."
– Alan C Middleton, US Academic

5 DON'T SATISFY YOUR CLIENTS!

Satisfied clients are the best kind, right? Wrong – wowed clients are what a successful brand should be built on. Don't focus on meeting your clients' needs. Focus on exceeding their expectations. Deliver more value than they expect, and then do it again.

Peugeot – A Brief Case Study

Meeting clients' expectations is the goal of most good businesses. However, great businesses routinely go above and beyond. They don't settle for meeting expectations, but really want to wow the customer. Peugeot is one such company.

When presented with the issue of providing robust, excellent customer service in a web-based environment, the automaker went to great lengths to determine what the optimum solution was and then amp it up a bit.

The result of their research was a partnership with a company that allowed Peugeot to answer every customer email or comment in a personalized way, without any need for automation or "canned" responses. In an age where automation seemingly reigns supreme, customers are taking notice of this.

Why the Wow Factor Is Vital

Every business has competitors. It doesn't matter what your products or services might be, there is at least one other company out there doing the same thing. What's more – you can bet that your competitors are doing many of the same things you are. That is, determining what your customers' needs are, how your products or services meet those needs and then engaging with those individuals.

There's the issue. Everyone's doing the same thing. It's a mass migration of a sort. You're lumped in with your competitors with no real way to stand out from the herd. By focusing on wowing your customers rather than just meeting their expectations, you gain the means to stand out from the mass of competitors and really gain notice.

How to Wow Them

When it comes to exceeding your customers' expectations, there are almost as many ways as there are business models. Different companies will take different steps to achieve this goal. Peugeot did this by achieving something that 99% of companies in the world never do – personal responses to emails and web queries.

That doesn't mean you need to do that in your own business. The steps you take should be based on factors specific to your business and your customers. For instance, if you only have a small web presence, then providing personalized responses to emails in a timely manner isn't really "wow-inducing".

You do have the means to determine exactly what steps or efforts will wow your customers and clients, though. During your niche branding, you determined what your customers needed and what problem your products or services solved for them. Simply take that to the next level and amplify the results. For instance, you might:

- Offer a lifetime warranty where other manufacturers only offer 30 days
- Offer deep discounts regularly to repeat customers

- Customize a product to individual customer needs
- Special order items on an as-needed basis for each customer

The list of possibilities is endless. Tailor your actions to your industry and your customers. Determine what their needs are, what expectations they hold and then go above and beyond for every customer.

Bobby Marhamat

"Identity is cause; brand is effect. And the strength of the former influences the strength of the latter."
– Larry Ackerman, The Identity Circle

6 HOW AUTHENTIC ARE YOU?

If you want to build your brand effectively and develop a reputation as an industry leader, then you need to be authentic. Authenticity is vital for branding – without authenticity, your brand will be weak, and your customers will be likely to pass over your company in favor of a more authentic competitor. How do you improve your brand's authenticity?

Apple – A Brief Case Study

We've already mentioned Apple previously, but the company is an excellent example of authenticity, even more so than Google and other obvious choices. Why is this? What is Apple synonymous with?

- Quality design
- Innovative engineering
- Forward thinking
- Constant improvement

Bobby Marhamat

When Apple announces a new product (iPad, iPhone, etc.), we generally expect the first production run for that product to sell out quickly. This is because the company has authenticity – their devoted customers and fans fully believe in Apple's products, in the company's drive for quality and innovation, because it does not deviate from that.

Certainly, some product designs and concepts are a bit less exciting than others, but they always improve, innovate and stay ahead of the pack. That's what their customer base has come to expect – and it's a core component of their brand.

What Is Authenticity?
Before we look at how you build authenticity into your company, you need to know what it actually means. It's a term taken from philosophy and psychology. Merriam-Webster defines authenticity as, "true to one's own personality, spirit or character". From that, we can begin to draw parallels with your business.

Generally, authenticity confers a sense of truthfulness of origins, of originality, sincerity and straightforward, honest intentions. It also conveys a sense of leadership in accordance with internal values, rather than external values. Therein lies one of the keys to how this concept applies to your business.

Stand for Something
A company that customers deem as authentic stands for something. It holds true to inner guiding principles. The company practices what it preaches. To reference Apple yet again, the company preaches innovation and ingenuity. They also go to great lengths to practice those tenets, as well.

Your company must do the same thing – you don't have to focus on unique design if you're

38

not a manufacturer, but you need to ensure that your company holds true to its inner, guiding principles rather than being swayed by external forces. Customers want to do business with authentic companies, companies they see as safe or unambiguous. They want to do business with a company with a defined reputation, integrity and clear goals that match their own experiences.

Core Factors in Authenticity

Fostering a sense of authenticity within your company is essential, but it can be difficult to do if you're unsure what metrics go into the process. We've talked about authenticity being tied to core principles and integrity, but it's also much more. To boost your brand's authenticity, you need to focus on certain aspects, including:

- **Originality** – Originality ties into your company's ability to bring your customers something new, different and unique. Even if you're selling the same type of product as another company, it must stand out as original and unique. For example, both Nike and Reebok manufacture athletic shoes, but both bring something unique to their customers via their products.

- **Your Company Story** – Your brand should have an authentic story. You might think of this as "heritage" or "origin", but it all boils down to the same thing. Where did your company come from? Why was it born? What did you, the business owner, launch the company to achieve? Let your original story shine through in everything your business does, from product selection to customer service.

- **Real Use/Value** – Also known as utility, this core concept focuses on what you bring to your customers. Your products or services should be such that they offer something your customers can't live without or don't want to do without. Look once more at Apple's range of products and you'll see this core concept in action.

- **Core Beliefs** – As mentioned previously, your company must have inner, guiding principles or beliefs. Those beliefs need to be tied into the very fabric of your brand. Examples of this include a dedication to building real relationships with each customer, honesty and forthrightness, integrity, benefiting the environment and more. These tell your customers that your business wants to achieve something greater than just making money.

- **The Genuine Article** – You might be more familiar with this quality as "sincerity", but the concept is the same. You need to ensure that your brand is genuine and earnest. Your company should strive to uphold the highest standards in terms of product performance or service quality, customer experience and customer satisfaction. Being genuine ensures that you are not seen as just another faceless company out to make a quick buck.

- **Awareness** – The level of awareness within the general public of your brand is vitally important. The better known your company is, the better your brand recognition and authenticity will be. However, that doesn't necessarily mean that you need to be an internationally recognized brand – local businesses can develop immense authenticity right in their hometown. The local pizza parlor where all the locals go for great food and fun, or the bakery downtown renowned all over town for having the best baked goods are perfect examples of this.

- **Growth** – Authenticity is tied to brand growth in a way. The more your customers see your brand becoming known with other people, the greater your growth and momentum will be. And this ties neatly to the belief that well-known companies are more authentic than those that no one has ever heard of. Would you be more willing to buy a product from HP or from some no-name generic computer company? Most people would choose HP.

Bobby Marhamat

"The future belongs to brands that do more than pay lip service to real dialogue and recognise that their customers want them to believe in something."
– James Murdoch, Chairman/CEO, News Corporation, Europe and Asia

7 THE PERCEPTION OF QUALITY

Quality – it's one of the hallmarks of a good brand. No matter what you sell, from widgets to tree removal service, quality is imperative, there is simply no substitute for it. However, it goes beyond actual service or product quality, longevity and performance. You have to foster the perception of quality in your customers and prospective customers in order to build your brand effectively.

Nissan – A Brief Case Study

One of the world's best-known automakers, Nissan products haven't always been perceived as being of high quality. In order to improve their perceived quality and value, the company took dramatic steps. These steps focused on seeing quality issues from their customers' point of view and ultimately resulted in the creation of several Field Quality Centers.

Each center is dedicated to reproducing and rectifying actual customer complaints regarding vehicle problems, performance issues and component failure. By providing a quick response and taking each complaint seriously, Nissan was able to improve their brand's perceived value overall.

What Is Perceived Quality?

It's important to understand that perceived quality differs considerably from actual quality. Your products might have very high quality, but if your customers perceive a different value, it makes little difference. Perception is the key; perception is everything.

43

The Business Dictionary defines perceived quality as, "A consumer's opinion of a product or brand's ability to fulfill his or her expectations. It may have little or nothing to do with the actual excellence of the product and is based on the firm's or brand's current public image, consumers' experience with the firm's other products and the influence of opinion leaders, consumer peer groups and others."

That's a mouthful, but what it really means is that your brand or product's perceived quality doesn't necessarily hinge on anything inherent. It can change based on what others say about your company or your offerings, as well as with individual consumer experiences with your company or products.

Improving Perceived Quality – Altering Perceptions

As mentioned, your company's perceived quality may have nothing to do with your actual quality. "Perceived" is the key word there. In order to build an effect brand, you have to ensure that you are creating the right perception of your company, and that you take immediate steps to rectify any negative perceptions that may exist.

- Substance First – Before you can improve the perception of quality, there has to be real quality to your substance. Both your company and your products or services must have high value for consumers. It's generally not possible to create a perception of high quality where there is no quality to begin with.

  Substance comes first. Make sure that your company and your products offer quality in every way possible, and then work toward changing perceptions. Often, this process leads to integral changes within your company, manufacturing processes or product line to help boost substance and inherent quality.

- Change Areas That Matter – Your customers' only care about things that affect them directly. Therefore, any changes to your company that improve quality but that don't impact customers won't alter your perceived quality.

  For instance, if you create a change in your company that greatly improves production time, but doesn't translate to immediately visible benefits for your customers, their perceptions won't change. If you want to engender a brand reputation of high quality, then all changes need to affect your customers.

- Understand Quality Cues – Chances are good that your customers are basing their quality determination on only a few factors. It's also equally likely that you are focusing on changing the right cues.

  Before you take any steps to alter perceived brand quality, make certain that you know what factors matter most to your customers and which ones they're using in their determination of company quality. Doing otherwise is little more than a waste of time, money and effort.

Bobby Marhamat

"Brand" had been with us since human time began. Millennia before marketing coined the term "branding," the how, when, and why of people "attaching" to a person, product, or idea, has been nothing less than the engine of history."
– Bob Deutsch, President, Brain Sells

8 PROMOTE THE INDUSTRY

Leading brands are able to promote their industry, and then create a new category within that industry that allows them to stand out from their competitors. By promoting your industry, you help build brand recognition tied to something larger than yourself, but you also build a platform to boost your branding efforts.

Microsoft – A Brief Case Study

When it comes to industry promotion, there are few companies that hold a candle to Microsoft. The company doesn't manufacture computers. It doesn't make peripherals. But for all that it doesn't do, it's one of the best-known brands in the world. Why is this?

Take a look at Microsoft's website and you'll start to see why. Interspersed with their software offerings, you'll find links that promote the industry. Take the launch of Windows 8, for example.

Of course, you can download the operating system directly from the website, but Microsoft also goes to great lengths to encourage customers to find the perfect computer for their needs from a variety of different manufacturers. You'll find Acer, HP, Dell and other companies listed as partners – success for Microsoft requires that their partners are successful.

How Do You Promote Your Industry While Still Promoting Yourself?

It can seem very difficult to promote your industry without glossing over your company. For instance, if you manufactured performance accessories for automobiles, you wouldn't want to promote other companies that offer the same products. There's good news, though – you can promote your industry while still promoting yourself.

While Microsoft is a very good example of this, another company that you should take note of is Monster Energy, the energy drink leader. The company makes a wide range of drinks designed to provide more energy, boost performance and more.

They are also heavily involved in industry promotion – not the energy drink industry, but the extreme sports industry (as well as others). The company actually has their hand in several different markets, from heavy metal music to video games and extreme sports.

Through events, features, industry performances, shows, interviews and activities, Monster promotes others and is in turn promoted, allowing them to cement their dominance in the energy drink world (only a handful of energy drink companies have as pervasive a brand, with Red Bull and Rockstar being two exceptions).

So, what does that mean for you? Simply put, you need to become involved in the industry. For example, if your company manufacturers or sells athletic clothing, sponsor local events, high school sports teams, or consider becoming involved with training in some way. If your company is an auto dealership, consider getting into the performance scene, or sponsoring classic car shows.

There are myriad ways that you can become more involved in the industry without actively promoting your competitors. But why would you want to do this?

Building Your Brand within Your Industry

The benefits of promoting your industry should be obvious, but let's look at the situation in a bit more depth. The single largest reason for promoting your industry is for brand recognition and identity. By actively promoting your industry, you tell customers and potential customers unambiguously where your company stands, what it's about and that you're dedicated to promoting others. That's an essential quality these days.

You must understand that consumers are increasingly dissatisfied doing business with faceless corporations after nothing but profit. They want to see companies that are dedicated to promoting success unrelated to more than themselves and concerned with being supportive and sharing. By promoting your industry, you do exactly that.

In addition, when you take an active hand in promoting your industry, you are able to build your own niche and stand out. Look again at the efforts of Monster Energy and how those efforts have translated into their success. If it weren't for their immense support, chances are good that they would be far less known.

Bobby Marhamat

"A brand is more than a trademark. It is a trustmark. A brand is a covenant between the company and the consumer. A trusted brand is a genuine asset."
– Larry Light, US Brand Consultant

9   WHAT'S YOUR NAME?

What's in a name? According to Shakespeare, not so much, "a rose by any other name would smell as sweet". However, the Bard was never involved in branding, and his advice, while sound for other areas and for the philosopher in all of us, should be avoided completely by businesses hoping to build their brand.

Your name is one of the most essential things to recognition and brand success. The right name offers a steppingstone to better branding. The wrong name can leave you wallowing in anonymity.

Hollywood – A Brief Case Study

Hollywood actors and actresses are famous for changing their names to something with more appeal to the general public. How many of the names below do you recognize?

- Marion Michael Morrison
- Cherilyn Sarkisian
- William Michael Albert Broad
- Maurice Micklewhite
- Declan MacManus
- Patsy McClenny
- William Henry Pratt

Now, compare those to their Hollywood names – you'll likely recognize most of these:

- John Wayne
- Cher
- Billy Idol
- Michael Caine
- Elvis Costello
- Morgan Fairchild
- Boris Karloff

Why did these stars change their names? They did it for better recognition, to make it easier to remember and for its "star" power. For instance, which name sounds better to you – Patsy Mc-Clenny or Morgan Fairchild? Which is easier to remember, William Michael Albert Broad or Billy Idol? The same considerations apply to your business.

Name Considerations

Whether you're creating a name for your company, your brand or your product, you need to keep several rules in mind. Following these guidelines will ensure that you get maximum impact and traction out of your name, and that you are able to build the reputation, visibility and recognition you need.

1. **Keep It Positive** – Your name should conjure up positive images for your customers. However, you don't need to limit positivity to the word or words you choose. Fonts, colors and backgrounds can also add to a positive impact.

2. **Visually Appealing** – Your name and associated logo should not only be positive, but visually appealing. The colors, font choice, letter sizes and graphics should all tie to-

gether to create an appealing overall image that connects with your target audience. The Caterpillar (CAT) logo is a very good example of this – it's bold, strong and enduring, just like the company's heavy machinery.

3. **Unique** – Your name has to be unique to your company. Using a similar name (or the same name) as another company is a bad move. Not only does this create potential legal hazards for you, but it can give the impression to consumers that you're trying to rip-off someone else and capitalize on their success, rather than building your own. Make your name descriptive, suggestive and, most of all, unique.

4. **Brevity** – If you take a second look at the Hollywood stars who changed their names listed at the beginning of this chapter, you'll notice that many of them changed to something shorter. Short, sweet and to the point is essential.

It's hard for a consumer to remember your company if your name is four or five words long. "Robert's Handmade Jewelry and Bangles for the Family" is much less memorable than "Robert's Fine Jewelry" or even "Bob's Bangles". Keep your name as short as possible to maximize visibility and memorability.

Bobby Marhamat

"Passion and love for a brand and its consumers sustain us. For how can we ever devote our continued highest energy to something if we don't believe in it passionately?"
– John E Pepper, Chairman, P&G

10 KEEP YOUR EYE ON THE BALL

Focusing on your company's goals is vital, but maintaining that focus over the long term can be difficult, particularly when daily operations continually try to move your focus elsewhere. Still, it's essential that you focus on becoming the best of the best within your niche, and the way to do that is by developing and focusing on company goals.

Why Goal Setting Matters

Goal setting matters a great deal in all aspects of life, but particularly in the business world. Without goals, you have no means of measuring your progress toward success. Moreover, you might not have any idea of what success really looks like. Even worse, you may have no clear idea of what achieving "success" is actually costing your company in the long term.

So, goal setting is both a means of measuring progress and a yardstick to measure costs. It can also be a vital tool for fostering even more growth – think of it like fertilizer for your company. By having specific goals, you boost morale, improve your processes and can make necessary changes to any activities, efforts or processes as you go.

The Steps to Goal Setting

If you've been in the business world for any length of time, chances are good that you've heard the acronym SMART when referring to goal setting. This refers to a specific system of setting goals that have particular characteristics. It's important that you know these and how they apply to not only your goals, but to your overall branding efforts and becoming the best of the best within your niche.

S: Specific

Your goals need to be as specific as possible. If necessary, break larger goals down into smaller sub-goals that add to each other until you've reached a larger one. For instance, rather than setting a goal of being more profitable, you should set a goal of earning $X in the first quarter of the new fiscal year.

M: Measurable

Goals must be measurable, or they're not attainable. To use the example above, you can easily measure the progress toward reaching a set dollar amount for the first quarter of the year. If progress toward your goals cannot be measured, then they need to be more specific.

A: Attainable

Of course, your goals must be attainable – unattainable goals do you no good at all. In order for a goal to be attainable, it has to matter to your company and brand. If it doesn't hold value for you, you won't be able to achieve it. Keep your goals within reach, and be prepared to set a new goal as soon as you attain the first one.

R: Realistic

Realistic goals are those that can be reached, but are not necessarily easy. Often, this requires developing a plan on how you will reach your goals, and then implementing that plan (reaching that goal may require a list of other, smaller goals).

T: Timely

Any goals you set must have a timeframe during which you have to achieve them. It might be a week, or even a year, but you have to have a timeframe for achieving those goals, or you will find yourself unable to maintain your commitment. Avoid vague and undefined and create a schedule.

By setting SMART goals for your business, you ensure that you are able to grow your brand. Of course, those goals have to be in line with your business, and should help promote and establish your company within your niche. By remaining focused on reaching one goal after another, growth becomes more a matter of course than a mystifying process that eludes you.

Bobby Marhamat

"Brands are built from within; any chief executive worth their salt knows it, but it remains an uncomfortable truth for most marketing departments. Brands, in practice, have very little to do with promises made through advertising. They're all about promises met by employees."
– Ian Buckingham, Founder, Bring Yourself 2 Work

11 DONT BE SHY

You are not alone in your industry, and you'll find a wealth of other businesses in related verticals. It's important that you aren't shy about recommending other businesses to your customers. Not only does that provide help to your customers who need something other than what you offer, but it helps grow fellowship with other companies, fostering greater success for all.

The Truth about Networking

Recommending other businesses is really what networking is all about. This applies to more than just social media networking with sites like LinkedIn. Networking in the real world offers tremendous benefits for your branding efforts and your overall success.

How does it work?

Essentially, networking is nothing more than forming loose alliances with other companies in related verticals. For instance, if you sell organic produce, you might ally yourself with a company that sells and installs solar panels, or one that sells organic fertilizer. If your company deals with sign printing, you might ally yourself with an installation company that offers commercial exterior sign mounting and installation.

Every business in every niche within every industry on the planet has potential allies. By recommending those allies to your customers, you are able to achieve two things.

1. You build fellowship with other businesses and encourage them to the do the same thing for you. By not being shy about promoting your partners, you help ensure that they will send customers your way as well.

2. You tell your customers that your brand is about more than just making a profit. You establish that your company is about supporting others, about growing connections and about helping your customers even if you don't have the products or services they need.

In short, you enhance your brand while inspiring confidence and trust.

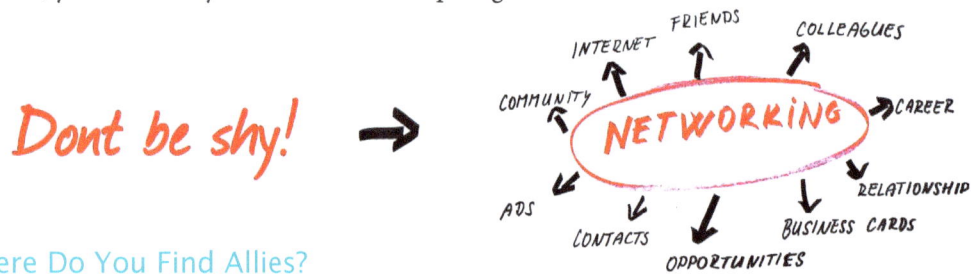

Dont be shy! →

NETWORKING — FRIENDS, COLLEAGUES, CAREER, RELATIONSHIP, BUSINESS CARDS, OPPORTUNITIES, CONTACTS, ADS, COMMUNITY, INTERNET

Where Do You Find Allies?

While your company most certainly has potential allies out there, it can be hard to find them. After all, your main focus should be on building your brand to be the best in your niche and reaching your goals. However, you can find potential allies through a variety of ways, including:

- Your local Chamber of Commerce
- Local business mixers
- Local luncheons for business owners
- Social networking sites like LinkedIn
- Industry newsletters, magazines and other periodicals
- Speaking with your customers

"One can often trace the sources of a brand personality—here it is the advertising, there the pack, somewhere else some physical element of the product. Of course, the personality is clearest and strongest when all the elements are consistent."
– Stephen King, Former JWT Executive

12   PEOPLE REMEMBER BRANDS, NOT COMPANIES

What companies supply the components for Apple's iPad? What companies supply Nike? What companies have a hand in manufacturing that big screen TV in your living room? Chances are good that you have very little idea. But it's a sure bet you remember the other names – Apple, Nike, Toshiba, Samsung and other powerful brands. This is because those companies have gone beyond being mere "companies" and have built a brand. People remember brands. They forget companies.

Ralph Lauren – A Brief Case Study

Polo is one of the most recognizable brands in the world. In fact, more people remember the Polo name than the company behind it – Ralph Lauren, though there's significant company recognition here as well. However, we need to look no farther than the iconic polo player logo on Ralph Lauren clothing items to see the power of a brand.

What's the first thing you think of when you see that logo (wherever it might be, from clothing to cologne)? You think "Polo" with a capital P. You think brand, not company. You can add that power to your own business by building the right brand.

Be Memorable, Not Forgettable

If your brand is forgettable, or you lack a recognizable brand at all, you're in for some serious problems. You must focus on creating a memorable, recognizable brand that evokes the right emotional reaction in your customers or clients. How do we do that, though?

1. **Use Your Brand in All Areas** – One of the first things you'll want to do is ensure that you're using your brand name and logo in all areas, from direct mail marketing to in-store signage. The more visible your brand is, the more recognizable it will become for your customers.

2. **Educate Your Audience** – You cannot expect your audience to instantly realize why your brand is superior to your competitors. You need to educate them. Remember, you can't do this by hitting them over the head with a sales message. Take the time to educate your potential customers with accurate, viable information, comparisons and data designed to be easily read and digested (but omit the "BUY NOW" message).

3. **Make Your Brand Interesting** – If your brand isn't interesting, it's forgettable. But how do you make it interesting? There are numerous ways to accomplish this. Consider developing your own mobile app that offers value to your customers and that is tied to your brand.

   Engage with customers and potential customers through social media like Twitter. Develop informational content that offers value to current and potential customers – value that goes beyond your brand, but ties directly with it.

4. **Foster a Community** – Building a community around your brand is important, but it can be confusing. One way to start growing that community is by recommending other businesses to your clients (as mentioned in the previous chapter).

   Yet another option is to create a group or club for your most loyal customers that offers rewards they value (note that this doesn't mean that it holds value to you – value to your customers is the rule). You can also foster community through mobile apps, through SMS marketing (as long as it's not invasive) and by becoming more involved in your industry.

Use an Evocative Image and Wording

In the case study that opened up this chapter, we touched on the Polo logo used by Ralph Lauren. Take a moment and think about that logo. It's simple. It's clean. It's tremendously suggestive, and it's memorable. You need a logo for your brand that offers the same benefits (we'll get deeper into logo design in a later chapter). However, you cannot afford to have an uninteresting, uninspired or overly complicated logo.

A good logo can incorporate any number of elements, from graphic design to typography (and it should). Regardless of how many different design elements, it is a cohesive whole. Finally, that logo needs to be used everywhere your brand can be found, from your website to your Facebook page to your store's front door and signage.

Taglines are also important for business branding. Not all companies use taglines in their logos, but they can be very helpful. Simply put, a tagline differs from your mission statement, but still connects the reader to the core concept of your brand.

One of the best examples of this is one used by Apple several years ago – "Think different." Another excellent example can be drawn from Coca-Cola – "Life tastes good." Finally, HP's tagline "Invent" was both suggestive and compelling for customers.

Careful planning of your logo and tagline will help reinforce your brand's message every time your customers see them.

"Brand is a valuable asset of the corporation, and should be treated like any other asset. This means it must be invested in, put to work to generate value and held accountable for the results."
– Joanna Seddon, EVP, Millward Brown

Bobby Marhamat

13 DO NOT DILUTE

Your brand identity must stay the same at all times. If your company attempts to be different things to different people, you're doing nothing more than diluting your brand, which in reality is just tossing out all your hard work to build your brand in the first place. Hold firm to your brand identity and do not dilute your efforts.

Virgin – A Brief Case Study

Most people are familiar with Virgin, at least to some extent. This Great Britain-based company has extended its reach into multiple areas, from air travel to railways to space flight and even vodka. At first, things seemed to go well enough for the giant corporation, but problems quickly arose. The company had to sell off its music-recording arm to help fund the struggling airline division, and their venture into the railway service in England was a dismal flop.

However, perhaps the most important lesson learned from Virgin comes from the confusion on the part of potential customers. When you hear the name Virgin, it's difficult to tell exactly what part of the company you're talking about. This is brand dilution – confusion regarding what a company offers, what they can do and what their company is about can be very, very damaging. While that damage was mitigated to an extent in the case of Virgin (the company is simply too large for brand dilution to be a "killer"), smaller companies will find that diluting their brand can ultimately lead to total confusion, chaos and even failure.

66

Dilution from Over Extension

There are several ways you can dilute your brand. Perhaps the most common is trying to do too much, to be all things to all people. The sports metaphor is to play within yourself, and resist the temptation to try to do more than you can. For instance, let's say that you have built a strong brand via a product. Your brand is doing so well that you decide to launch another product that's completely different from your original base. The problem here is that the new product isn't quite as high quality as the original (inferior products exacerbate brand dilution).

As your brand becomes more and more diluted, you'll find that your profit margins fall across the board, both on the new product and on your original one. Customers pay a premium price for products from a company they trust (a company with a strong brand). When that brand's value becomes diluted, they're no longer willing to pay the same high premiums and go elsewhere, leading to a loss of profitability. It all snowballs, leading to a distressing downward spiral that could potentially leave your company devastated.

Don't Dilute

The key thing to remember here is that you cannot afford to be everything to everyone. Focus on building your brand in one area and then slowly grow into other, related areas if possible. Extension to other areas should always come only after very careful consideration. In addition, extension should be to:

- High quality products to avoid issues of inferiority
- Into related areas that can tie directly into your original brand/product
- Into areas that strengthen your core brand

Of course, there are plenty of examples of companies that have over extended themselves and tried to be too many things to too many different people. On the other hand, there are those companies who are able to grow their product offering without diluting their brand. In essence, they are able to roll out new products under their original brand name, bolstering their success. Think of firms like:

- HP
- Black & Decker
- Apple
- GE (though the company had problems at one point)

Signs of Brand Dilution

How do you know if you're diluting your brand? Here are some signs to look for so you can turn the situation around before it becomes detrimental:

- Losing association with market segment
- Losing association with quality
- Losing association with product area

Build your brand to be the best in your niche. Over extension into other niches or even other industries can be the deathblow for even fabulously successful major companies. Avoid the temptation to reach too far and concentrate on building what you have.

BRAND BRAND BRAND BRAND

"What the nervous system is to the body, the brand is to a healthy organization."
– Terry Tyrell, Worldwide Chairman, Brand Union

14 BE CONSISTENT

Consistency across your brand is vital for long-term success and growth. If you are inconsistent, you will find that you lose customers easily. Inconsistency is a sign of instability – a sign that your company doesn't quite know itself. If you don't know yourself, how can you serve your customers? Consistency, however, must be distinguished from repetition – repetitive statements and restatements only alienate your audience further. Consistency is creating a pattern, but not necessarily repeating the same messages over and over.

Nike – A Brief Case Study

When it comes to consistency in branding, few companies can really hold a candle to Nike. In fact, the company is also a poster child for being incredibly consistent without being repetitive. The most important factor in their consistency is the placement of their logo in everything, regardless of the marketing message, the advertising medium or the presence of their products. In fact, some of their most effective marketing efforts haven't focused on their product at all, but on their message and on including their logo. The company uses their logo everywhere, regardless. It has become synonymous with their brand – you only need to see "the swoosh" to understand not only who is behind the message, but to understand the lifestyle evoked by the brand.

Being Consistent in Your Branding

It can be tempting to think that consistency is the same thing as repetition. Doesn't being consistent mean being repetitive? Actually, that's untrue. Consistency doesn't have to have anything to do with repetition, and in this day of ephemeral marketing media, repetitive statements can actually lose you your audience.

But if that's the case, how can you be consistent?

Take a page out of Nike's playbook. Make sure your logo and tagline are used everywhere possible. The more visibility your logo has, the more your customers will begin to equate it with your brand. Eventually, they'll only have to see the logo to be immediately immersed in your brand.

Create the Right Logo

Logos are a lot like clothes for a brand – they're powerful images, stylish and should be changed only when necessary. But what goes into creating a good logo? Actually, it's surprisingly simple, though it should be approached with care. What's more, having a good logo is vital for being consistent in your branding efforts.

Your logo should:

- **Be distinctive** – Don't follow the herd. Make your logo yours alone and unique.
- **Be communicative of your brand and quality** – Your logo should immediately evoke your brand's values and quality in the minds of your customers.
- **Be appropriate** – Appropriate logo design ensures that it connects with your target audience on their level (think Toys R Us, with their fun, childlike font and colorful design).
- **Be timely and timeless** – While logo refreshes will happen, your logo design shouldn't be changed on a daily basis.
- **Be versatile** – Versatility in design ensures that your logo can be used across the spectrum of multiple platforms, enhancing consistency.
- **Convey and stay true to your intended message** – Your logo should tie into both your brand and your intended audience.

Bobby Marhamat

- **Be simple** – Simplicity ensures that your brand is identifiable everywhere, boosting consistency.

For some excellent examples of logo design, think about IBM, UPS, Apple, Nike and McDonald's. If you are unable to create your own logo (and most business owners cannot), hire a professional to get it right the first time.

Logo Color Considerations

The colors you use in conjunction with your logo and company name are very, very important. You might think they're little more than a way to add some "pop", but it goes far beyond this. Colors actually summon specific emotional responses in the viewer, and you want to use colors that reinforce your brand's values, quality and overall message. This is just as important to consistency as using your logo in everything you do.

Given the importance of color choice, you should know a few things about what types of emotional response various colors can evoke. Here's a quick rundown:

- **Red** – Passion, excitement and boldness
- **Orange** – Retro, friendliness and warmth
- **Yellow** – Cheerfulness, freshness, spring and summer
- **Green** – Health and wellness, trustworthiness, natural and earthy
- **Blue** – Trust, smart, stability, authority and soothing
- **Purple** – Eclectic, fun, feminine, stylish
- **Brown** – Warm, professional, retro

Regardless of the colors you ultimately choose, make sure that your logo can be used across all mediums in both full color and black and white/grayscale. This provides maximum utility and consistency everywhere.

More Than the Logo – Maintain Your Brand's Consistency

Your logo design and color choice will have a huge impact on your ability to remain consistent throughout your marketing and branding efforts, but there's more to it. Ensure that all branding efforts are also consistent in promoting your company's culture and values. For instance, you cannot have two different personas on Facebook and Twitter.

A customer should have the same experience in terms of brand values, ethics, culture and personality regardless of where or how they interact with you. The rule of consistency applies to all outlets, from Facebook to flyers, Twitter to in-person visits at your physical store. Ensure that your brand is consistent at all times, so that your customers can connect with you.

Bobby Marhamat

"In daily practice, the word brand stands as a surrogate for the word reputation. In fact, your brand acts just like a person. When you know a person's reputation, you can predict his or her behavior. You know what that person is likely to do or say—or not do or say—in any given situation. Your brand works the same way."
– Jim Mullen, Founder, Mullen Advertising

15 REBRAND - REBUILDING YOUR IMAGE

Your brand is essentially your company's personality. It's what your customers know about your company. It tells them how your business will act and what they should expect. In fact, your brand is your reputation. Just like reputations, there may come a time when your brand becomes sullied – rebranding can help rebuild your reputation and foster greater trust with your customers. When should you rebrand?

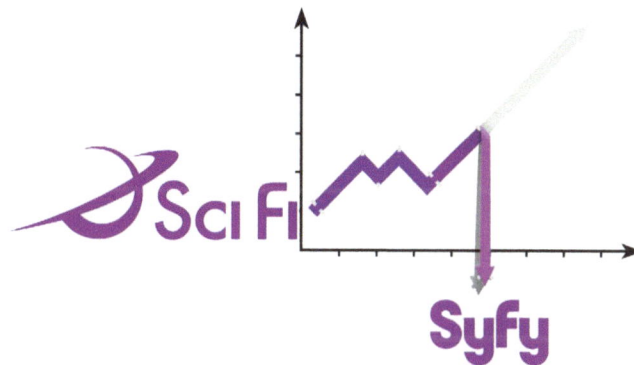

Syfy – A Brief Case Study

The SciFi Channel has always been something of an underdog, due in large part to the nature of their programming, their target audience and the myriad of viewing choices. For all that, the company wanted something they could call their own – they were unable to trademark "sci-fi". Through a poll of their audience, they decided to go with an alternate spelling of their name that could be trademarked – Syfy.

Beyond the ownership issue, the company also wanted to connect with tech-savvy viewers and boost their brand's image in terms of hipness. Sadly, it backfired. There have been few rebranding efforts that resulted in greater negativity or ridicule. Rebranding is sometimes vital, but it can be dangerous, particularly if you go about it the wrong way.

When Is Rebranding Necessary?

Given the importance of brand (it's your company's personality and public face, after all), it's vital that you know when and how to go about rebranding. When is it necessary? Why would a company need to rebrand at all?

Actually, there are many different reasons for corporate rebranding, including the following:

- Financial issues such as bankruptcy or corporate restructuring often result in rebranding.
- The need to eliminate a negative image or negative connotations associated with a brand can necessitate rebranding.
- An increase in competition and a greater need to stand out from the crowd can demand rebranding.
- Reduced market share and profitability can also cause the need to rebrand a company in order to increase meaning to your audience and rebuild market share.
- The transition required by a change in leadership can also necessitate rebranding so that the company reflects the new personality.
- When there's a need for greater relevance, a "light rebranding" or brand refresh is usually undertaken. This differs from full rebranding, but offers many of the same benefits.
- If your company and another merge, you'll find that there's a considerable need to rebrand, to ensure that your brand carries sufficient weight with the other company's audience. Each situation is unique, but bear in mind that when this happens, resist the

temptation to throw the baby out with the bath water.

Do It Right or Don't Do It At All

The world is full of rebranding horror stories. Syfy might be one of the most infamous recent tales of woe, but they're far from the only one. Others include the 2009 Tropicana rebrand debacle, the bizarre logo for the 2012 London Olympics that had the world up in arms, the Andersen Consulting/Accenture disaster and Pepsi's $1 million logo redesign failure.

What lessons can we derive from these startling failures?

When it comes to rebranding, do it right or don't do it at all. Rebranding should never be undertaken lightly. Even brand refreshes should be carefully calculated to ensure that you don't lose or sacrifice your target audience. If you're still not convinced of the need for caution, consider these potential pitfalls of rebranding:

- Shifting your brand away from values your audience cares about
- Loss of a familiar name with no carryover to the new name (think Accenture)
- Lack of meaning for your audience with new names or logo designs
- A lack of clarity involving brand identity, personality and culture
- The potential for rejection, derision and anger from your audience (think Syfy)
- A lack of clarity in your market position

Bobby Marhamat

"Predictability, it turns out, is what makes a brand fit with consumer expectations and keeps it profitable."
– Robert Passikoff, President, Brand Keys, Inc.

16 NOW LET'S BUILD YOUR BRAND

Now that you understand what your brand should be, the advantages and benefits good branding offers and the importance of avoiding tarnishing your reputation, it's time to look at how to build your brand. This chapter will look at how you should pull the whole thing together to create a seamless brand that conveys personality, culture and quality.

It Starts Internally

The first step in building your brand is ensuring that you have the inherent quality necessary to really make it in today's competitive environment. Look at every aspect of your business, from product quality and longevity to customer service. If there's a lack of quality anywhere in that chain, no amount of branding will do you much good. Low quality will always trump good branding.

79

Beyond ensuring that the necessary quality is there, you need to do a few other things internally, before you do any type of brand building.

- Ensure you understand your company's value proposition to your customers so it can play a central role in your branding.
- Ensure you understand your company's ethics and culture. If you seem to be lacking in these areas, it's time to go back to the drawing board. You cannot afford to have an impersonal, generalist brand. Specificity, company culture, ethics and value all play an essential role in good branding.
- Ensure you know whom your target audience is and how to reach them.
- Ensure you know how your product solves your customers' problems – it's all about them, really, not about you or your company. Focus on serving your customers, not on growing your business.

Other Important Considerations

In addition to the items listed above, there are quite a few other elements that go into defining your brand so that you can promote it. These include:

- Where will your product stand in pricing compared to comparable products from your competitors?
- How can you network with related companies within your industry to benefit from fellowship?
- What is your company's unique personality? Are you casual and laid back? Are you professional and polished? Are you environmentally minded? Are you international and multicultural? Your brand needs to embody these qualities and convey that impression to your audience.
- What is your product's position and how does your company stand out from competi-

tors? What makes you unique? Why should your customers choose you over someone else?

- How will you reach your target audience? Close consumer contact is essential for branding success.
- What's your company name and how does it boost your brand? What does it translate to in other languages? Never forget the lesson Chevy taught the world about the importance of naming research when the Nova flopped in Spanish-speaking markets.
- Does your brand name complement or highlight core values of the company?
- Is your brand relevant to your customers' lifestyles? Think of how Monster Energy connects with their audience by fitting into their active lifestyle and promising the ability to do more. Think of how Gatorade connects with their audience's lifestyle.
- Can you partner with a related company to add additional benefits for your audience? Betty Crocker and Hershey's joint products are a perfect illustration of collaborative efforts that expand both the potential market and the benefit to customers.
- How will you remain consistent across all mediums and outlets? How will you combine your company's name, logo and personality into a seamless whole that communicates effectively with your target audience?
- Remember to stay focused on becoming the best within your niche. Avoid brand dilution by overreaching.
- Identify and locate partners to help you spread your message – partners should have complementary skills, expertise and connections to a wider audience.
- Remember that the goal of branding is to have a brand that people know and connect with. It's not about direct sales. It's all about building relationships.

Bobby Marhamat

"People are more willing to buy branded goods provided they are persuaded that they are getting value from them. And they need to be convinced of those benefits, in authentic everyday language, without being confronted by corporate-speak. Get it right, and you create a virtuous circle. Get it wrong, and you get punished for it."
– Andrew Curry, Director, The Futures Company

17 STEPS TO TAKE WHEN CREATING A NEW COMPANY

Building a new company from scratch can be a lengthy, frustrating process. Ensuring that your brand shines through in all elements of that new company is vital. This chapter will give you a systematic look at what you should do when creating a new business and brand.

Product

Your product is the most important part of your new company. Whether you're selling a physical product (shoes, clothing, cars) or an intangible one (insurance, telephone service, Internet service), your product must offer value, quality and performance.

Other qualities you should ensure are present are durability, longevity and cost effectiveness over time. Often, the best companies are built on the best products – don't leap directly into business building or branding. Ensure you have the right product first.

Create a Business Plan

A business plan is a formal document that outlines what your company does, where it's going and what you hope to achieve over time. These documents are essential for companies in need of funding – any bank will require you submit a full business plan (or at least a full outline) in order to be considered for any type of loans (including SBA loans). Even if you don't need startup funding, having a business plan will help your business stay on track with and ensure that you're growing according to your plans.

Name

Your company's name will be a huge component of your brand. Good naming practices require that a business name is:

- Short
- Memorable
- Pronounceable
- Informs the audience of the business' purpose and has meaning
- Does not have negative connotations in international markets or other languages
- Original and not similar to any competitor's name

Logo

Don't cut corners here. You'll need a good logo for your business. Make sure you enlist the help of a specialist who can understand your brand and design a logo that ties into your branding efforts and your company's personality and culture.

The right logo should be simple, effective, evocative, memorable and able to be used in all mediums and platforms. That includes using it online, in physical marketing collateral and in signage. Choose effective colors for your logo that create the emotional response you want from your audience, but also make sure that it works equally well in color, black and white and grayscale.

Create a Tagline

Taglines are not required for businesses to be successful, and plenty of companies don't have one, but they can complement in countless ways. There are many advantages to be gained with a good, effective tagline, particularly when it comes to branding and telling your customers who you are and what your company's about. Study taglines used by today's most successful companies and create one that is simple, succinct and relates directly to your brand.

Build a Web Presence

These days, no company should be without a web presence, and this goes far beyond just having a website. Of course, your website should be welcoming, informative, entertaining and tied into your brand, but you also have to take the same considerations with your social media accounts and your blog.

Each component of your online presence should reflect the same personality and brand to your customers. Use your logo effectively across all platforms and ensure that communication with customers is in the same voice. Tie your logo's colors into those platforms as well. In all aspects of web interaction, be real, be consistent and be authentic.

Make sure you brand your online outlets correctly. This goes beyond the profile picture used on Facebook or the description of your company on Twitter. It requires that you have the right account and domain names as well. Ideally, you'll use your company name for all of these. This ensures that your customers can find you more easily, and it also helps prevent your competitors from hijacking your identity to divert traffic away from you.

CONCLUSION

Building a brand is vital for your company to succeed.

However, doing that can be harder than most people believe. It requires considerable information, the right action steps and knowledge all too often gained only through experience (and not always the positive kind).

Whether you're building a local business or one that will sell products internationally, your branding efforts are essential to your ultimate success. Creating the right brand can be confusing, but with the right steps and the right information, you can build one that accurately reflects your company's personality, culture and ethics.

Remember – your company's brand is more than a vague, fleeting mystical concept. Your brand is your company's public face. It's your personality. It's your reputation. Your brand goes far beyond your marketing materials, beyond your products and beyond your customer service. While all of those are vital components of your brand, it's quite a bit more than this.

With the right branding efforts, you can position your company correctly and connect with your target audience. You gain immense benefits by creating a brand that consumers trust and recognize; a brand that they empathize with and actually want to bring into their businesses, their homes and their lives.

Done right, branding is an immensely powerful tool.

Done incorrectly, it can lead to disaster.

This book was conceived with a simple goal: To provide you with the understanding and tools necessary to go about branding the right way and reap the benefits that your business deserves.

It walks you through branding from the basics of determining what branding actually is to ways to build expertise. It teaches the elements of branding, how to determine a niche focus and how to exceed customer expectations and build a reputation for excellence. This guide helps you learn how to communicate with a target audience, how to avoid the direct-sell faux pas and what metrics real customers use to determine a company's quality (or lack thereof).

From the importance of social media to building authenticity within your industry, from naming to logo design, you are now the expert in branding.

Cheers!

$16.95

ISBN 978-0-615-74780-4

51695>

9 780615 747804

Bobby Marhamat

THE "B" WORD

www.ingramcontent.com/pod-product-compliance
Lightning Source LLC
Chambersburg PA
CBHW060802270326
41926CB00002B/61